Pebble® Plus

Wonderful World of Reading

Let's Go to the Library

by Martha E. H. Rustad

Consulting Editor: Gail Saunders-Smith, PhD

Consultant: JoAnne DeLurey Reed, Librarian and Teacher
Scroggins Elementary School, Houston, Texas

CAPSTONE PRESS
a capstone imprint

Pebble Plus Books are published by Capstone Press,
1710 Roe Crest Drive, North Mankato, Minnesota 56003.
www.capstonepub.com

Library of Congress Cataloging-in-Publication Data
Rustad, Martha E. H. (Martha Elizabeth Hillman), 1975–
  Let's go to the library / by Martha E. H. Rustad.
      pages cm.—(Pebble plus. Wonderful world of reading)
  Includes bibliographical references and index.
  ISBN 978-1-62065-093-6 (library binding)
  ISBN 978-1-4765-1740-7 (eBook PDF)
1. Libraries—Juvenile literature. I. Title.
Z665.5.R87 2013
027—dc23
                                    2012030347

Editorial Credits
Erika L. Shores, editor; Veronica Scott, designer; Marcie Spence, media researcher; Laura Manthe, production specialist

Photo Credits
Alamy Images: Jeff Greenberg, 11; Capstone Studio: Karon Dubke, 5; Corbis: Dann Tardiff/LWA, 17, Kim Jongbeom/TongRo Images, 21, Rick Gayle, 13, Shalom Ormsby/Blend Images, 7, 9; Shutterstock: Dmitriy Shironosov, 19, Login, design element, Rob Marmion, 15, SharonPhoto, cover (library), ZouZou, cover (child)

Note to Parents and Teachers

The Wonderful World of Reading series supports Common Core State Standards for Language Arts related to craft and structure, to text types and writing purpose, and to research for building and presenting knowledge. This book describes and illustrates a trip to the library. The images support early readers in understanding the text. The repetition of words and phrases helps early readers learn new words. This book also introduces early readers to subject-specific vocabulary words, which are defined in the Glossary section. Early readers may need assistance to read some words and to use the Table of Contents, Glossary, Read More, Internet Sites, and Index sections of the book.

Printed in the United States of America in North Mankato, Minnesota.
092012   006933CGS13

TABLE OF CONTENTS

Library Trip

When I need a book

or a movie, where can I go?

To the library!

What else will we find there?

Librarians

"Which president had the most pets?"

"What's the biggest snake?"

People ask librarians questions.

Librarians are experts at finding

materials to answer hard questions.

FREE SUMMER READING PROGRA

Librarians are always busy.
They teach students how to
tell if Web sites are correct.
They help students use
online encyclopedias.

Librarians plan story times.
A visiting author reads
his newest book. We might
see a puppet show. In March
we celebrate Dr. Seuss's birthday!

Materials

We see rows and rows
of books filling the library.

Fiction books tell stories.

Nonfiction books tell facts.

We'll find movies and music too.

Computers

Computers help us find books. Type "dogs." The call number is 636. Find the shelf with that number. The shelf holds many dog books.

People use libraries for more than books. We look up facts on Web sites. We play computer games that teach reading skills.

Manners at the Library

A library is a place

for good manners.

We use quiet voices.

We are careful with library books

and return them on time.

I found my library books!

I'm checking them out.

See you at the library soon!

Glossary

author—a person who writes a book

call number—a group of letters and numbers that tell where a book is in the library; the call number is printed on a sticker on the spine of a book

encyclopedia—a book or an online collection that tells facts about many subjects

expert—a person with great skill or a lot of knowledge in something

fiction—books that tell stories that are not true

librarian—a person who works in a library

material—one of the items people may look at in libraries or check out of libraries; books, movies, magazines, and newspapers are library materials

nonfiction—books that tell facts that are true

Web site—a place people can go on the World Wide Web

Read More

Kawa, Katie. *My First Trip to the Library.* My First Adventures. New York: Gareth Stevens Pub., 2012.

Keogh, Josie. *A Trip to the Library.* My Community. New York: PowerKids Press, 2013.

Rustad, Martha E. H. *Reading Is Everywhere.* Wonderful World of Reading. North Mankato, Minn.: Capstone Press, 2013.

Internet Sites

FactHound offers a safe, fun way to find Internet sites related to this book. All of the sites on FactHound have been researched by our staff.

Here's all you do:

Visit *www.facthound.com*

Type in this code: 9781620650936

Index

Word Count: 198
Grade: 1
Early-Intervention Level: 21